Holding Things Together

www.chuckoneilauthor.com

Holding Things Together

ISBN: 978-1-7321708-6-5 (paperback)
ISBN: 978-1-7321708-7-2 (ebook)
Library of Congress Control Number: 2020948979

Cover Art: Watercolor, Frank LaVanco, 1948

StoneBear Publishing LLC - 11/2020
Milford, PA 18337
www.stonebearpublishing.com

Also by Chuck O'Neil

The Perfect Scar

Eating Out

Beyond Basilicas

SAWKILL FALLS EDITIONS

The Falls of the Sawkill
19th Century
Artist: Signature Illegible

for Celeste

for Ben, Chuck, Beth, Sarah

HOLDING THINGS TOGETHER

Chuck O'Neil

CONTENTS

Going 2

1

First Names 6
The Borough 8
Streetscape 10
Looking Out 12
Film Festival Matinee 15
Liberty Hill 17
The Corner 18
Plans And Elevations 23
Kid Outside 24
River Road 25

2

November 28
Cliff Walk 30
September Son 31
Pears 32
Now as Then 34
Seeing 36
Visiting After Thanksgiving 39
Mother Daughter 41
Wedding 44
Borrowed Light 46
Bell in the Breeze 48
Our Front Walk 50

3

Naming the Needs   52

Oak   54

Thaw   57

Fretwork   58

Cash Flow   60

Waiting For A Lumber Truck   62

Money Enough   65

Waylaid   67

For The Ones To Come   69

September 10th 2001   70

Provisions   72

4

Jake   76

Reckoning From The Steps   78

Godspeed   79

Catching A Breath   80

After   82

Yardwork   83

The Present   84

Bell Path   86

Voice   87

West   88

Magnificat   90

Walking Distance   92

Easter   93

Last Morning   First Light   94

Notes   96

Acknowledgements   100

About the Author   101

HOLDING THINGS TOGETHER

Our settlements in the beginning were coastal
mostly: Built up where rivers widened into bays,
deep enough for the ships that carried us here
from other lands.

Journal Entry, 1683

Going

It's this way:
being captured is beside the point,
the point is not to surrender.

Nazim Hikmet

Trans. Randy Blasing & Mutlu Konuk

Through my cell's small window
(A hole really

Where the builders omitted two stones)
I saw birds fly

One morning   fog lifting
Not hearing the usual shouts

Or the usual boots
I suspected my captors had gone

I crouched to the slot in my door
Saw light along the jamb

Pushed slightly   the light widened
Pushed   the slab swung free

From the battlements
I could see across the lake

Vineyards   mountains
Clouds making their way

And that night   stars far up
Lights around the shore

By sunrise
I'd raised the windows I could raise

And when I left
I left that place to the weather

Once   from a distance
I looked back

And the sun
Flared the turrets like steeples

1

For the inhabitants
This day   and before   and yet to come

First Names
John Biddis   1749-1820

That summer   in August
    my settlement
By then a good-sized port
    was stricken with the fever

Death swept house-to-house
    like fire in a stiff wind
Yet   unlike so many others
    I was able to remove myself

My wife   my small children
    to lands I'd been told about
Up the river
    a fair distance to the north

Good air   rushing water
    hills rife with timber
A fine benchland there   the entirety of which
    I acquired before long

And built our cottage
    a mill   later a village
Laid out like my native city
    with straight alleys and straight streets

6

The son of immigrants
    I named this place   this outpost
For a town across the ocean
    where my ancestors lived

And   that their names might remain
    we christened certain of the east-west streets
After our sons and daughters Anne Catharine
    George John Sarah Elizabeth

The Borough

I came to a village
Above a river
Hills all around it

The streets   wide by any measure
Were woven with alleys
Verged with trees in full leaf

And with architecture
Seldom seen standing together
In such a small town

And though I'd never
Passed those buildings before
I remembered them

And it seemed to me
I was always
From that place

I arrive today
As I arrived
Years ago

And recognize
Earlier villagers
As my kin

Their doorways before me
Rafters above me
Joists below me

Risers and treads to lift me
Railings they held once
To steady my step

I arrive by way of mortises and tenons
They've sawn and bit-braced
And fitted and pegged

All the handwork
Living in the buildings
Holding things together

Streetscape

Surely there is something more
in each of the trees . . .
Walt Whitman
from 'Song at Sunset'

Through the window
A work on paper

Charcoal by a local artist
An eye for
Streets before snow

The same grain and gray
Found in Historical Society prints
Hereabouts years ago

Unpaved in those days
And the yard across the way
Fenced waist-high
With ornamental iron

Maples   leafless   in rows
Already the borough appears
Lived-in many lifetimes

10

A similar linework now
Though the ancestor's
Fence is gone

Though that corner building
With the second story porch
(An inn   the caption says)
Went up in flames

The same names for streets
The same daylong dusk

And sycamores
Wintering out there
Standing for those early hand-drawn maples

Looking Out

for Tom Hoff   for Dick Snyder

It's a question of seeing
So much clearer

Of doing to things
What light does to them
                    Guillevic

                    Translation by Denise Levertov

Mid-November   late July

Who can say

How it is

Looking out a window

Drawn there by the light

Long slant of it

Across the wide street

Painter's light

The way   with shadow

Light sheds light

Over bluestone and brick

Over casings   plinths   quoins

As it blackens the glass

And steeps the brackets

Beneath the eaves in shade

12

And some nights
Who can say
How it was
With moonlight
By these entrances
These same sash

For souls who came before
Held for a time
Between the lintels and the sills

Wondering what to make
Of such glow
Of the way light migrates
Over all that was
Lifted into place
Lived in
And handed down

And how is it now
That those who are gone
Who it seems
Were just here
Are in town yet

Shedding light still
Long slant of it
Across the clapboard

Angling the alley   the walkway
The bench   the bollard   the verge
The planter   streetlamp   sign

Long light
Bridging the buildings
Sweeping the trees

Film Festival Matinee

The seats in our historic theater
Are original for sure

Probably there never was a way
To get comfortable in them

(Tough somehow
Even on the knees)

But likely the best in town once
When   between two wars

They bolted them
To this sloped floor

And addressed them
With these brass tags

Maple arms   cast-iron frames
Ascetical almost

Out-of-style   such stiffness
To the lot of us now

Who shift as the lights dim
And settle in

Where bodies before us
Have left impressions

Liberty Hill

We took down trees
That threatened the house

Smoothed off the bluff
From which they pitched

And opened it up
To sunlight

Bluebirds
The ridge across the river

We wore a path in time
Along our new verge

And sat in our bodies
And looked out in time from this rock

Innisfree   our little bit of it   anyway
This hilly reach above the streets

Spirit of it   the flowered rise
That rose within us

The Corner

. . . nothing is truly mine
except my name. I only
borrowed this dust.
        Stanley Kunitz
        from *Passing Through*

1. Postcard   *late 1800s*

We see you
There on the corner
In an earlier century

The newly-built courthouse
The old stone jail
Behind you

Not long
After our national war
Not so long
Before the World War

Fall
By the look of the trees
Afternoon
By the spill of the shadows

And light enough still
For the postcard photographer

18

Who's stood his camera
In the dirt middle of High Street
Lens leveled to the west
Vanishing point in the hill
At the end of the road
Rutted then   empty at that hour

Except for
The good-sized wagon
Hitched to the curb   (yours?)

And except   by luck   for you
Standing like any one of us
Hands in your coat
Staring down the years

2. Monument   *1931*

We see so many of you
Gathered on the corner
To dedicate the monument
For soldiers and sailors

Fourth of July   after a light rain
The courthouse
The old stone jail
Behind you

19

Not long
After the World War
And not so long (though you couldn't have known it)
Before the next one

Among you there   the Governor
A local man   man of his time
Mustached   rail-thin   statesmanlike
Hands by his side while speaking
From the bluestone top step
Of the ones who served
Of his hope for peace
From now on

And afterwards   smiling
In the photo with August Kiel
'The Marble King'   fellow townsman
Whose idea the memorial was
Who made a gift of it to the County

The benediction pronounced
By Reverend Arob
Taps played
By Louise Mulvaney
('star trumpeter'   'a slip of a girl')
Three veterans of the World War
Allen Meyers   Lee Thursby   Clarence McIlveen

Fire the salute
And the east corner of Centre Square
Becomes remembering ground

3. Today

We stand now
Where you stood
With the weather as it is
The courthouse
And the old stone jail
Behind us   as behind you then

Not so long
After Korea   Vietnam   The Gulf
Afghanistan   Iraq
And possibly not long
Before a flare-up somewhere else

Flags lowered
The wreath placed
Heads uncovered

We recognize
The town around us
Its hills   streams   river

And each of us
A dwelling place
For the Missing   the Unknowns
The ones who came home

We see ourselves
Keepers in our time
Of this corner
These names

Memorial Day, 2017
Milford, Pennsylvania

Plans and Elevations

Bless the house
A cottage really
Low ceilings   moonstruck windows
Pale hill rising behind it

And all the houses

And the full names
Of those who winter in them tonight
And the wintering ones before
And the ones still to come

Bless the porches
Dormers   gable ends
And let grief drift past the railings
And suffering lift away like smoke

Praise the plans and elevations
That outlast
That stand here
In the middle of a week
At the end of a year
Above ground
Open to the weather

Kid Outside

for W.S. Merwin

You lived for years
During your boyhood
Not so far west of these hills

A Pennsylvania coal town
In a slump by then
With no end in sight
Where your father was sent
To shepherd Presbyterian souls

Where   weeks before flowers
You heard 'church-goers'
Returning to the northern lakes
Honking through the anthracite sky
Like the flock above me now

Liturgy on the fly
And you   a kid outside
The church on Washburn Street
Looking up

24

River Road

for Paul McNeil

All finite things reveal their infinitude
Roethke

You saw early on
How the road begins
North of us

Where the river begins
Where water from the lake
Tumbles together
With water from the hills

And how one road
Threads the interior
And winds down
Along our drop-offs   rapids   wide pools

And levels up with the falls
And the sometimes-flooded fields
And scrolls through the oaks
And switchbacks as it rises above the ledges

From the overlook
Good Friend   the rain gone
May you see the whole of it

The town clear across the valley
The sun's rose streamers in the west

And may you see
The way you came
And the way now
Beside the river
Your road runs on

2

November
for Celeste

The two of us
Cruising down the gravel drive
In that pumpkin-colored German car
We borrowed for the week
Nothing to our names
'Just Married' squiggled in shaving cream
Well-wishers waving us off
Shifting   beeping   waving back

Remember how it poured that night
The whole way out to the shore
Getting lost twice
Checking in late to the harbor hotel
And next morning
Racing up the coast to catch the ferry

Remember the island ghosting into view
How the headlands rose
How gray air gave way to blue
The first cottages
And the heaven
Of jetties and narrow streets
All to ourselves

November again   Love
Leaves all down
The light we love easing in
And a sense the world's ending
A sense we're starting out   as before
From weather to weather
For richer for poorer
Well-wishers waving
The two of us
Leaving the mainland

Cliff Walk

Young   the man and woman
College-age maybe   not much more

Traces of their faces
In the faces of four small children
(Two boys   two girls)
Who stand with them
On the overlook hedged with bayberry

Summer day   Newport sky
All six smiling together on *three*
Where the walkway curves along the cliffs
Long green lawns on one side
Ocean below on the other

It munches underfoot
And runs on in shadow and sun
Beyond the border of this old photograph
And draws their eyes from rise to rise
One living wonder to another

September Son

One of the boys
One no bigger than anybody out there
Always catches his eye

Who sizes things up on the run
Who uses his head
To finesse the white ball down the long green field

Golden hour
Late-day sun combusting trees
Flaring ledges

A son somersaulting
Leaping up
Chasing the glare through the shadow of the valley

Pears

An old woman
Handling pears
Her purse in the cart behind her

My mother there
In a similar coat
(Who'd by then lost

Her husband   her hair to chemo
Too much of her eyesight)
Calling   crying   to say

Her purse had been stolen
In the produce section
Or maybe by the deli

She said she felt
She was being
Punished for something

So I stay by the lettuce
Keep watch
While she puts pears

In a clear bag
Lowers it beside the carrots
The bread   the limes

Looks at her list
Then moves ahead
A little at a time

Now as Then

for Cecelia O'Neil

We were there

We saw the world you saw
And we saw it
Before we could see it
For ourselves

Stone steps   sloped walkway
The old two-story above the river
Sheared granite banks below
Its rapids choked with boulders

We were mesmerized that day in July
The very moment you were
By a greenish-yellowish bird
No bigger than a dragon fly
As it whirred from branch to bush to rain barrel
Looking for anything red

At night
When you lay in the too-crowded upstairs room
We heard the train with your ears
As it thundered through the trestle
It clattered   wracked   clanged   blew its stack

34

Boomed through the ravine
Shook the timbers
Rattled the windows   the dishes

And after the last
Metal-to-metal clack
We fell back asleep
To the sound of the falls
Tumbling the gorge downstream

With you those mornings
When you walked so far
To the school on the hill

When you left lunch
On the sill for your father
A loom-fixer at the mill

With you now
As then
As it must have been   Mother

You kept us close
Before you could call us
Before you gave us our names

Seeing

1
I see him in the dark
Coat over his pajamas
Wheeling trash cans
Out toward the streetlight
Feeling his way along the bricks

A last job as it happens
For one who once ran jobs
With ten to twenty men
Who was (Mom said on the phone that night)
Still in the driveway
Taking forever

For whom a day later
The ambulance came
His tool belt on a hook
In the back hall closet
Planner wrapped with rubber bands
Wallet doubled up on the dresser

His papers 'to take on the city'
Stacked downstairs on the pool table
With those sketches
For that getaway in Vermont

36

Who lived his life
In a single New England town
And left
The same winter month he was born
Not a mile from where he came into it

I see him early on
The narrow house   that steep street
Just two turns up from the cathedral

All eyes those days
Learning from the others
Little by little

2
I see him under the light
Ammonia smell of the blueprints
Cedar smell of the colored pencils
He sharpens as he goes

And watch him   in his work clothes still
Getting ready for tomorrow at the kitchen table
Drawing yellow red green lines
Along the brass edge of the wood ruler

37

Laying down the conduit
He'll bend   couple   and bury
Beneath soon-to-be-poured concrete floors

To this day I hear him
Whispering to the plans
And follow the press of his pencil
On a ragged scroll
He stuffed in the rafters of the garage

And follow him up steel stairs
(Prints rolled under his arm)
To the not-yet-glassed-in upper stories

Follow now too in the flow
Of fathers   uncles   sons
Strong backs   mechanic's hands
Each with a knack
For 'running the show'
Scaling lengths   minding alignments
Mapping the next day under a light

Visiting After Thanksgiving
for Tim

They buzz you in
Through electric doors
To get where he is kept
While they overhaul
His meds again

Bringing him
The turkey-cranberry-stuffing sandwich
Is no problem
But tea in a glass bottle's verboten
So they pour it into a hospital tumbler
(Blue bears doing a samba around the side)

Your friend was once
In great spirits near the ocean
Wiffle-ball games on the beach
The clam bar   the cottage

And you'd suggest
If this far inland such a thing could be arranged
That they permit him a sea's sapphire sky
And Jesus   at night
Those salt breezes off the bay

More wish than suggestion
For one whose mind is
Misfiring around the holidays
Who's stalled now with the others
On hodgepodged furniture
TV across the way
Spitting images

Mother Daughter
for Celeste   12.12.12

Today   as you know
(You whom I've never seen
Or spoken to
Except in these old photos)
Today's your daughter's birthday
Your only girl

All smiles in that oval frame
Across the room   Brownie uniform
Just getting over the mumps   you'll recall
Offering a cookie to the military man
On the sofa beside her   her father
Smiling also   also in uniform

She's a woman in this picture
And older than you would ever become
Standing on the porch with her girls
Bride   mother of the bride   maid of honor
Beautiful   can you see

These boys by the fireplace
Are your handsome grandsons
Good brothers   good sons
Good grown men now

Not long ago
On a sweltering June afternoon
I (your son-in-law   by the way
Of course you know)
Snapped this little series of her
Smiling in Bishop's Garden
Where she played as a child
Among the boxwoods and red geraniums

And here   across the wide D.C. street
In front of the brick house
Where she grew up
Where you last lived   Mary Ann
Where   she told me
You once made curtains
Out of sheer parachute silk

Your daughter's birthday
And everyone's here
And everything is as it is
And we live where we live above the river
Plant red geraniums
Grow our own boxwoods

And on given days
The faces we've placed in frames

Make themselves known
As you do sometimes
When your daughter laughs
And   out of the blue   discovers herself
Laughing your laugh

Wedding

They declare their love
In the open
Face to face
They give their word

Everyone is lifted up
Everyone sees
The light of one
In the light of the other

Second selves
Of the avenues and cross-streets
Sunstruck bridges   landmarks at night

Second nature
The mirror lake   the moonlit river
Of the kingdom of heaven
Within the other

Seeing them together
Everyone sees
There's no two like them

How easily they live in their bodies
Carry earlier stories

44

Earlier shoulders   earlier hands
A way of standing
The shape of a mouth
Earlier hearts   earlier eyes

And   seeing them together
Everyone can see
How it is

How those who couldn't be here
Who passed themselves on
And passed on
Are here

How those to come
Have saved this date too
Mystical witnesses
Jubilant   taking it all in

for Ben and Jordan
St. Petersburg, Florida
June 4th, 2011

Borrowed Light

Morning sun
Runs uphill along the snow
Streams beyond belief among the trees
And the same sun spills
Through bars of borrowed light
Across the floor

Everyone knows the light
When they see it
Passing through glass

Everyone knows how the moon
Can shine like the sun
And roads glow in the dark
How a man will find his way
East to west across the rivers
And a woman find her way
North to south along the coast

Both living their histories
Following signs as they go
Both knowing by eye
The day they've arrived

They see each other
And they know it

As the eye delights
In light over snow
And knows the place beyond landscape
So they see each other
And know where they are

And the same sun moves
From room to room within them
And awakens the pictures
And slants alongside shadow
Through the open doorways

They know the light
When they see it
And they lift up the light
In each other

Daily light
Handed down
To the heart of things

for Chuck and Noa
Palm Springs, California
May 3rd, 2013

Bell in the Breeze

May there be
A clearing
A little rise always

From which
You glimpse
Your life together

As the moon follows the sun
Above your small town
Rimmed with hills

While light
Runs down the hollow
Out across the lake

As water
Falls and falls
Beneath the footbridge

May the kin
Living within
Lift you

May loved ones
Prepare a path
Upslope through the trees

And may the day
Come in full
And call you

From a stairwell
A window
Between buildings

Out of the blue almost
A bell in the breeze
Waking you

One to the other

for Sarah and Quint
Milford, Pennsylvania
August 12th 2017

Our Front Walk

for Lily   Rory   Patrick

The forms ran out from our steps
And tee'd into other forms set along the street
And the pours were spread
Over one summer   after the war
When everyone was building things

Dad got home   and Uncle Walt drove up
His truck's massive drum in a slow spin
Stirring the 'mouthful of mud'
He'd saved for us from some big job

The mix ticked   trickled
Spilled down the chute
A glop-stone soup
Dripping   slapping   splattering
As they worked it to the corners with shovels

They sawed the screed back and forth
Floated and troweled and tooled the edges
They pulled the coarse push broom
Across the stiffening surface
And tarped the new section in case of rain
Weighting it in place with old bricks

Dusk almost by then
Forever ago now

3

A man has to live, if he would not founder and go to the bottom and not make his port at all, by dead reckoning.

Thoreau

Walden
from *Where I Lived, And What I Lived For*

Naming the Needs

Men
Men who are woodworkers
Would rather be building something

So we keep shop meetings
To a minimum
Half an hour once a month
More than this
It begins to feel like therapy

Last Tuesday
Our list included forstner bits
A scoring blade for the Altendorf
A dozen two-foot clamps
And down the road
A better system for mortising locksets

We put our heads together
To compress a couple of deadlines
And as we got up to go back to work
Peter (last name Flynn) says
Maybe we need
To set up a phone on the shop floor
For times when everybody's
Gone from the office

52

John Yerrington (youngest of three
Adult sons with parents in their eighties) says
Given the noise
We'll need a light on the wall above it
Red prob'ly
That'll flash when it rings

All agreed
Some no doubt recalling
Mark O'Connell   his brother's crash
How Mark was
At his bench assembling doors
When he got the news

Oak

1

He drives early
To the lumberyard across the river
Where they've set out waist-high stacks
Of rift-and-quartered white oak

In the barrel-vaulted warehouse
Winter sun streaming through the skylights
It dawns on him
As it had dawned before when piling wood
That old Shaker saying
Hands to Work   Hearts to God

God of this unheated warehouse   he thinks
Of this heavy draft blown down from Ontario
Spiraling dust motes in shafts of light

And of the slap and echo
Of one slab clapping against another
Like a kneeler dropping in a cathedral

God of the sliver
He bites out with his teeth
And of the single bird aloft in the collar-ties

2

Almost noon
By the time he loads up
Leaves the lumberyard
And stops at the Quick Mart
For tea   two donuts   the paper

God as well   he figures
Of the twenty-car pileup on page seven
Of the high-walled hospital on the hill

And (slowing through the E-Z Pass
Accelerating toward the wide windblown bridge)
Lord too of the growth
They found to be the cause
Of a dear friend's headaches

3

Backed up to the shop door
He walks the oak across the first bay
Falls into the rhythm
Of his hands again

Low sun floods the windows
Spills over mouldings and sheet goods

55

Over the shaper table
And every hand tool in its path

4

And when the others go
He makes the rounds through the long rooms
Benches and machinery all still
As if listening

It's the hour
When rosewood panels
Sleep in the press
When the carcass parts of cabinets
Lie with their frame members

Everything blanketed with a fine dust

He stands in the bluish half-dark
Furnace firing-up downstairs
Metal roof ticking in the wind

Thaw

The time of year
You picture signatures   go-aheads
Checks floating in

The way our pond must feel now
Recovering water birds
Reflecting more sky

And uphill   flush with brick-red buds
The way our oak trees
Must be feeling

New work in the book
And the sun spending daylight all over town
And everyone feeling forgiven again

Fretwork

A delivery of cabinetry
Philadelphia circa 1780

We'd watched the weather for days

Each one that morning
(There were four of us)
Walked to the shop from where he lived

We covered our belt buckles
When lifting our work into the long cart
Most of it made from mahogany
And finished the color of tobacco

We centered the load as the sun rose
Stuffed it   tarped it   tied it off
Hung our tools over the side

Good it was a May morning
Good the horse drew the load slow
To the high streets across town
Views of the river   trees in rows
Transoms   sidelights   brass everywhere

Good too how the owner left word for us
To use the main staircase
As the back stairs were narrow

58

And had winders
And the main stairs were deep in tread
Gentle in rise

The room down the hall was a fine space
Tall windows   oak floors
Rose marble fireplace

We fixed the bedrails
To the head and footboard
Placed the nightstand for the chamber pot
And the bookshelf and the blanket box

We set the lower chest between the windows
Raised the upper atop the lower
Soaped the runners   slid in the drawers
And crowned the chest-on-chest
With its pediment   carved urn   carved flowers
Cut-and-carved fretwork
Webbing up under a scrolled cornice

We stood in the room
And looked at all we'd shaped
Then collected our tools
Swept up our dust
And left the house and the high streets
The air outside almost fall-like
Some daylight still ahead of us

Cash Flow

We worked off and on for Paddy
(From Kilkenny   I think he said
Came over with the Beatles and Stones)
Living by then for years in the Bronx

He sputtered GC lingo
In his accent
Which took time
To get the hang of

And was known to 'sip the sauce'
Some days getting an early start
So every job I made sure
The last payment was COD

One morning   middle of February
I deliver study cabinetry
To the East Side   between Lex and 3rd
Cherry with corduroy glass in the uppers

Paddy's guys (younger versions
Of himself   just hairier) waiting there
On the street when I arrive
And we unload   muscle everything in

To the service elevator
To the 8th floor
Where   a tad flushed
Paddy's pacing the site

Says he's got my check
But has it hidden
Somewhere in the apartment
I'm double-parked   I tell him

Better get lookin' then   he chuckles
I'll tell you when
You're gettin' warm
And in no time

I'm in the bedroom
The dresser   second drawer down
Pulling a check for over three grand
Out of a pair of plumb-colored panties

Paddy cracks up
In tears
Might actually fall over
His guys howling like it's high school

And me laughing later driving up the Thruway
All smiles pulling into the bank

Waiting for a Lumber Truck

Middle of August
Sitting on a wall in the shade
And waiting for a lumber truck

We (both of us
Long-time small-time
Business owners) chew the fat
About how tough
Things continue to be

Never really
Said much before this
Job-talk here and there

So I'm caught off-guard
When he says
This country's done

The whole thing   I ask

Pretty much
Unless there's a revolution

Yeah   I say
Chase the moneychangers

Out of the temple

Hell he says
I mean buy all the guns
You can get your hands on
And while you're at it
All the silver too
Buy silver and bury it

In the ground
Like treasure I ask

Absolutely

But what if you
Get a head injury or something
And forget where you put it

Make a map he says
Make a map and tell two people you trust
(Sounding like someone
Who'd already done it)

Christ just comes out of my mouth

Yeah well trust me he says
It's over this country's done
Look at the signs

He starts spouting signs
As the flatbed rolls up   backs in
Beeps down the driveway   dust flying

We hop off the wall
And I kid him
Sounds like end-times   Bill
Maybe you should
Get the owner of this place
To build a fallout shelter

You laugh   he says
But just wait

Money Enough

Yesterday   on the way
Back from break   Drew said

One of the first things he'd do
When he won the lottery was

Write out a list of all those
He'd tell to go 'pound sand'

(Drew was a wizard with euphemism
Ran in the family   he said)

That list would be
Long as his arm

And once he'd taken his lump sum
He'd most-definitely quit this job

Pick up a Camaro
Hyper Blue Metallic

Get a pool table
With a bar in the cellar

Tickets to Mets games
Diamonds   and a shelf-load of shoes

For Lucy   who stayed with him
When things were less than stellar

Yeah   he said   money enough
To lubricate   take the edge off

And when the spirit moved
Groove down the road   settle old scores

Waylaid

It was just after mailing some bills
Feeling   as they say
A day late and a dollar short

When outside on the steps
I found fifty bucks   riffling there
In the stiff November breeze

I picked it up quick
Slipped it 'down south'
Into my pants pocket

But back in the truck's
When I saw it was
(Just my luck)   a fake

Its maker asking
In some faux monetary font
If I was disappointed

Declaring I wouldn't be
If I'd let Jesus Christ
Become the Lord of my life

And writing in the space
Where a famous American face should've been
Citing John Chapter Three   Romans Ten

Hard to believe the One
Known for those loaves and fishes
Got a good look at this

Especially for souls
In our neck of the woods
Folks here pretty much making do

Mending ways the best they can
Yet most days ending up
Feeling waylaid

For the Ones to Come

May you feel less shipwrecked
To think of us like you now
Watching whitecaps chop the bay

And   given coastal weather
May you grow
More gull-like by the day

Feathery   unfazed
When storm-seas
Plow through the pilings

September 10th 2001

A Monday   a workday
My birthday for the fifty-first time
I return calls   fly proposals
Schedule a delivery downriver

Windows open the whole afternoon
Upstate skies immense
Geese lifting off the pond
Wobbling up across the woods

We meet at the same restaurant
And when dessert comes
(A tartuffo drizzled with raspberry sauce)
It comes with a candle

Its flame doing a little jitterbug
The waiters hum-buzzing
Happy Birthday through kazoos
Everybody in the long room claps

Home early   and we embrace
The way those with a history
Of weekdays together can embrace
I close your book   turn out your light

Outside   the towering maple
The one the Tree Commission
Marked for removal
Waves its last leaves

I see the vacancy
No sapling can fill
Locust   beech   sycamore   oak
I dream the names like sheep

And picture limbs
Moonlit streets
A new Tuesday
Shifting shape while we sleep

Provisions

It'll happen
Most likely on a weekday

You'll be driving
To buy milk or bread
Or some other middle-of-the-week provisions

Your spouse
The one you've loved all these years
Will be getting the kids off to bed

Talk radio
God   that tragedy
Ten years ago already
You remember
It was a school morning

It hits
All over again
In the Cumberland Farms parking lot

From your car
You'd swear you were watching

An angel in a jogging suit
Paying for two cups of coffee
And a lottery ticket

You'd swear the cashier
With the long blue fingernails
Was divine

4

Jake

Across the new snow
I see him
Hobbling on a single hind leg
The other one
Dangling from his hip

And watch
As he engineers himself
Beneath our apple tree
Into something approaching a squat

Jake   the neighbor's arthritic dog
Gnarled tree
Crow frozen on a limb
Still Life in Winter Morning Sunlight

I call out to him   the crow flaps off
And eventually he makes it inside
Drops to the floor in his usual spot
A doorway between two offices

Jakey-boy   Jakey-boy   I whisper
Stroking his big dog face
And gently down the length of him

He seems mindful (if that's the word)
Of music filling the rooms
Hard to know
Whether Bach's *Magnificat*
Gives him consolation

Who never over the years
Appeared to be wondering
What is fair
Or what   if anything
Comes after this

Though it's clear
The way he
Twitches and whines in his dreams
He has wild imaginings

Reckoning From the Steps

As the neighbor's yard
Is all there is

For half-a-dozen
Guinea hens

Who've duckwalked into it
From the woods

So the field
Above the cemetery

Is   just now   all there is
For those three deer

Up in the open
Knee-deep in early corn

Godspeed

Hours yet till sunrise

You motor through the mist between towns
Straddle the skunk mound
High beam the greenhouse
And the corn-stalked edges of fields

Perfume season
When a buck will burst the brush
When insomniac raccoons
Find themselves
On the shoulders of secondary roads

You've been there
Moan of cars
Curves   long straightaways

Godspeed the animals
Shoeless   padding across macadam

Catching a Breath

A blur of fur
The squirrel hurls himself
One tree to the other

Dangles
From the thin end of a limb
Which whips like a fly rod

Little daredevil   he freefalls
To a thicker branch below
Scattering the few gold leaves that remain

He (I say he
Because his acrobatics seem so
Characteristic of a male on the make)

Puffs himself   twitches   chitters
Touches down lighter than a house cat
A few yards from my seat

And stands there
On hind legs   tail curling up
Cowl-like over his head

Front paws together
Above his pint-sized potbelly
In a kind of prayer pose

A breeze fluffs him now   just barely
And it barely lifts
The hair on my wrist

The two of us
Still as scultpure
Till the carpenter bee

Motors too close
Thinking I'm pine maybe
Or black spruce

I swat at him
The squirrel shoots off
And we're back

Creatures again
Jump-starting the hungers
Living in skin

After

Streets gone
Our birch on its knees

The late-season storm
Tapering to flurries now

(Beachtowns'll be
Shuddering by afternoon)

Flashlights drained
Books in a heap

Slate sky
Tingeing all of a sudden to blue

Yardwork

Somehow
It adds up

Daylilies weeks away
And hollies the deer mowed

To bundles of sticks
Showing their first ticks of green

Snow's likely still
The river could still spill

Here we are though
In a leftover March wind

Raking already
Clearing brushwood

The Present

Back from her
All-girls school reunion
She beeps
Speeds up the driveway
Kisses me   pops the trunk

Got you a present   she says
Needs TLC
But I picked it up
For half-off
Because of that

Pointing to one
Of the Buddha's hands
Missing a thumb
And this
Petting his chipped big toe

Love it   I tell her
Looks like he's lived a little
Yeah   she says
He'll fit right in
Around here

I leveled him up
Near the wall that afternoon
On a bluestone slab
Salvaged from
An old walkway

Where he's sat
A dozen seasons at least
Listing a bit to his left
Flaked in places
To his terra-cotta core

This morning
Up to his tailbone
In last night's surprise snow
Snow shoulders
Snow hat

Looking ok
Comical almost
Slight smile   eyes closed   all ears
Adrift
Holding his own

Bell Path

Our spit of earth along the slope
Finger of clay

Hill flowers
Above and below

Trees
Tall around us

Brownstone bench
On one end

Hive-shaped bell
On the other

Voice

May the one
Who is snow squall
River mist

Who made the moon
Toward which
All leaf smoke rises

Who's feather-covered
And winters for weeks
At our feeder

Let this one
Be the one within us
To give voice

West

Palm Canyon   2016

On foot
Desert heat
Not hard to picture this ancient terrain
Before there were names for things
Lunar
Mostly ledgerock and rubble then
With no path to speak of

And no clumped grasses
Or cactus or brush
Or low yellow flowers
No tall palms
Like the ones we see up ahead
(Blown in   they say
By the same coastal winds
That wear away
The outcroppings and the boulders)

And no theorem we know of
To solve for the likelihood
Of standing here together
Midway across this rock-littered arroyo

As some are just now
Rounding down to the canyon floor
And others move
In silhouette above us
Slow and steady along the rim

Magnificat

Sabbath-day breakers
Tumbling in   clawing back
The whole coast roaring

Wind without end
Motoring the red beach flags
Drifting dune sand
Across the wood steps

And few prospects
A handful of walkers
Holding their hats
A couple up the way
Leaning on the railing

So Jehovah's
Stationed by the pavilion
Collapse their pamphlet racks
And   hair and coats flying
Double-time it down the boardwalk

But Good News as is
(To my naked eye anyway)

Full-blown chapter and verse
This hurling surf
These gull gray skies

Walking Distance

May we live
The way the moon lives
In this coastal sky
The way
Down the shore tonight
Slow waves undo themselves

And all days
Be a path through the dunes
To the seaplace within

And live
The way the moon lives
Inland above this river
The way
Over soaked stones
The creek pours out into it

And all days
Be not far   Love
From living water

Easter

We go to the ocean
And stay in an upstairs room
With windows facing the water
And watch far off
As a trawler makes its way
Along the ink-blue rim of the world

And on our walk
Find ourselves
Marooned with all that has washed up
And not separate
From the shorebirds
Or the salt air
Or the risen sun

Last Morning   First Light
Vero Beach

Sea air   low waves
A pinkish-bluish upwash
Ahead of the sun

The beach birdless in both directions
And those palms along the shore
Barely swaying now

Only a comber so early
Beard   full-camo   headphones
Sweeping the sand for losses

Our loss (duffeled already
Among the older sorrows)

These ordinary days
This endland we've loved

Waking to light

Notes

First Names Pg.6

'That summer . . .' 1793. Philadelphia, a city of 50,000 and the
temporary capital of the United States, was ravaged by a yellow fever
epidemic. Thousands died. More than 20,000 fled, among them John
Biddis, who made his way 130 miles north to lands he purchased
along the Delaware River, which in 1796 he named Milford.

The Borough Pg.8

'I arrive today . . .' echoes an early Irish prayer called The Deer's Cry
(also known as St. Patrick's Breastplate), which begins: 'I arise today.'

Looking Out Pg.12

Tom Hoff, a founder of The Historic Preservation Trust of Pike
County, instrumental in establishing Milford's Historic Districts.

Dick Snyder, philanthropist, preservationist, a founder of the Milford
Enhancement Committee and the Greater Pike Community
Foundation.

The Corner Pg.18

East High Street Looking West Across Broad Street

Late 19th Century

Governor Gifford Pinchot

Speaking at the Dedication of the Soldiers and Sailors Memorial

July 4th, 1931

Upwards of 2,000 people were in attendance

Fretwork Pg.58

A reference to cabinetmaker Thomas Affleck (1740-1795).

Born in Aberdeen, Scotland. Immigrated to Philadelphia in 1763.

Waylaid Pg.65

John Chapter 3 (KJV): *Except a man be born again, he cannot see the kingdom of God.*

Romans 10 (KJV): *For whosoever shall call upon the name of the Lord shall be saved.*

The Present Pg.84

Acknowledgments

Thank you Eamon Grennan — friend, master-painter with the language — for those walks through the landscape and architecture of the Vassar campus, all the while catching up, sharing news about our families, our daily work, the world . . . For that morning we ducked into the archives to read through Elizabeth Bishop's manuscripts: what a gift to witness her great poems taking shape. I'm ever grateful for the tea and the time we spend reviewing my latest 'batch.'

Thank you Bill Kiger, President of the Historic Preservation Trust of Pike County, citizen by example, friend, and friend of poetry, who asked me to read some of the poems in this collection at The Trust's annual awards ceremonies.

The Columns Museum for help in researching the Soldiers and Sailors Memorial, its history and dedication.

The American Legion Post 139, Milford, Pennsylvania, and members of the veterans organizations who approved my reading of 'The Corner' on Memorial Day, 2017.

Thanks to local publications that saw fit to publish poems in this book: The Journal, Pike County Dispatch, Pike County Courier.

About The Author

Chuck O'Neil has written five poetry collections, most recently better gods. He lives in Milford, Pennsylvania, where he and his wife, Celeste, have lived since 1982. They have four children and three grandchildren. In 2022 he was named Poet Laureate of Milford.

Photo by Marie Liu

www.chuckoneilauthor.com

www.ingramcontent.com/pod-product-compliance
Lightning Source LLC
Chambersburg PA
CBHW030557130626
46552CB00006B/2576